Sarah Fox MD

Julie Stephenson

LITTLE CREEK PRESS™
A DIVISION OF KRISTIN MITCHELL DESIGN, LLC

Mineral Point, Wisconsin USA

Little Creek Press
A Division of Kristin Mitchell Design, LLC
5341 Sunny Ridge Road
Mineral Point, Wisconsin 53565

Book Design and Project Coordination: Little Creek Press

Book Photography: Julie Stephenson

Second Edition
January 2013

For more information or to order books:
email: info@superkidsbook.com
www.superkidsbook.com

Printed in Wisconsin, United States of America.

Library of Congress Control Number: 2012947449

ISBN-10: 0984924558
ISBN-13: 978-0-9849245-5-4

For our kids, Owen, Ella,
Sophia, Nolen and Lily, who inspire
us to make a difference.

·······················

And for our husbands, Trevor and
Ryan, for trusting us even though
we hide healthy stuff in
their food.

Introduction

Thanks for checking out *Super Snacks for Super Kids*. In this book, you will find a collection of simple snack recipes packed with the nutrition your kids need to feel energized throughout the day. All too often, the foods kids get for "snacks" are really "treats." As often as possible, encourage your kids to snack on healthy foods such as fruits, vegetables, and whole grains rather than junk food or sweets. Snacks should ideally include a fruit or vegetable and be something that provides the type of energy needed for their various activities. This book will help you meet your kids' needs so that they can be their super selves all day long.

We have included only recipes that are reasonable for busy families to prepare, with a basic set of ingredients that you should be able to find in most grocery stores. These recipes are meant to be a guide, not a script — you can make additions or modifications to help fit each recipe to your family's preference. We hope that this book will also spark your child's interest in helping in the kitchen. They are much more likely to try a new food if they have been involved in preparing it! If you teach healthy eating habits early, kids are more likely to make good choices on their own, building a foundation for lifelong wellness.

Scattered through the book, you'll find tips for choosing foods in the grocery store. The food industry has become very savvy and products are marketed in ways that make people believe that they are healthy. If you are new to reading labels, start out by trying to improve one product each time you go to the store. This does not have to be an immediate overhaul of your family's diet — you will get there over time.

In addition, at the end of the book, you'll find some recipe modifications to accommodate food allergies, and some explanations of special diets that you might encounter in your child's classmates.

Finally, our soapbox: whenever you can, eat real food. Avoid artificial sweeteners, processed foods, or foods that are naturally full of fat being turned into "low-fat" products. Get the real stuff and eat a wide variety of foods in moderation.

We hope you and your super kids love the recipes in this book as much as we do!

Happy snacking!
Sarah and Julie

Table of Contents

SUPER
SNACKS FOR
FOCUS

· ·

To learn and perform their best, super kids need
lots of protein and fiber to keep them full, and
healthy fats to help feed their brains.

8

Yogurt Parfait with Crispy Granola

Makes 1 serving

1/2 c. vanilla, plain, or greek yogurt

1/2 c. fruit (mango, raspberries, blueberries, or sliced strawberries)

1/2 c. granola (see below)

In a juice glass, place 1/4 c. plain or vanilla yogurt, top with 1/4 c. fruit, and 1/4 c. granola, repeat layers once more.

Crispy Granola:

Makes 8 servings

2 egg whites	Dash of salt
1/3 c. honey	3 c. old-fashioned oats
1 t. ground cinnamon	1/2 c. chopped pecans or other nuts (optional)
1 t. vanilla	1/2 c. raisins, dried cranberries, or other dried fruit (optional)

Preheat oven to 325 degrees. Spray a large baking sheet with non-stick cooking spray and set aside.

Put egg whites in large bowl and use a whisk or fork to mix until frothy. Stir in honey, cinnamon, vanilla, and salt. Add oats and nuts, if desired. Stir until oats are coated with egg mixture. Spread oat mixture evenly on baking sheet.

Bake 25 to 30 minutes or until golden brown, stirring mixture carefully every 5 or 6 minutes to prevent overbrowning.

Remove baking sheet to wire rack and stir in dried fruit, if desired. Cool completely until crispy and crunchy. Store in an airtight container. Freezes well.

Granola Bars

Makes 18 servings

2 c. old-fashioned oats

1/4 c. packed brown sugar

1/2 c. flax meal

3/4 t. cinnamon

1 c. whole wheat flour

3/4 t. salt

1 c. raisins or other dried fruit

1 egg, beaten

1/2 c. olive or canola oil

1/2 c. honey

2 t. vanilla extract

Preheat oven to 350 degrees. Line a 9 x 13 inch baking pan with parchment paper or spray with non-stick cooking spray. In a large bowl, mix together oats, brown sugar, flax meal, cinnamon, flour, salt, and raisins. Pour in oil, egg, honey, and vanilla. Mix together with hands and press into lined pan, leaving at least a half-inch border around the edge of the bars. If needed, use a rubber spatula or a piece of parchment to smooth out. Bake 22 minutes or until lightly brown on the edges. Pull the bars out of the pan with the edges of the paper and let cool for 5 minutes. Use a pizza cutter to cut into squares. Let cool completely and store in an airtight container.

Peanut Butter Pita Pockets

Makes 2 servings

1 apple, pear, banana, peach, or mango

1 medium whole wheat pita pocket

2 T. chunky peanut butter

Wash and cut fruit into 1/2 inch chunks.
Cut pita in half to make 2 pockets

Warm the pita pocket in the microwave for about 10 seconds to make it more flexible.

Carefully open each pocket and spread about 1 tablespoon of peanut butter on the inside walls of each pita half. You may need to warm the peanut butter in the microwave for a few seconds, especially if it has been in the refrigerator. Fill each pocket with sliced fruit. Serve at room temperature.

TIP: If you have bananas that are starting to turn brown, toss them in the freezer to use when needed for baking or for smoothies.

ABC Muffins

Makes 12 servings

1-1/4 c. whole wheat flour	1/2 c. mashed banana
1 c. old-fashioned oats	1/2 c. shredded carrots
1/4 c. flax meal	1/2 c. milk
1 t. baking powder	1/4 c. packed brown sugar
1/2 t. baking soda	1/2 c. olive or canola oil
1/2 t. cinnamon	1 egg
3/4 c. Easy Applesauce (page 86) or unsweetened applesauce	

Streusel:

2/3 c. oats	1 t. cinnamon
1/4 c. packed brown sugar	2 T. melted butter

Preheat oven to 400 degrees. Mix dry ingredients in a large mixing bowl. Mix remaining ingredients in a separate bowl and slowly add the dry mixture. Stir just until moistened. Pour batter into a greased muffin pan or use muffin cups. Mix streusel topping together with fingers. Before baking, sprinkle each muffin with streusel topping. Bake for 15-20 minutes until lightly browned. Let cool and store in an airtight container or freeze.

TIP: Old-fashioned (also called "rolled") oats are unprocessed oats, and are very good sources of protein and fiber. "Quick-cook oats" are old-fashioned oats that are chopped more finely. This exposes more of their surface area, so they absorb water more quickly. You can substitute quick-cooking oats for old-fashioned oats in baked recipes, but the texture will be more dense than with the unprocessed oats.

Blueberry Banana Muffins

Makes 12 servings

3/4 c. frozen blueberries

1 egg, beaten

3/4 c. mashed banana (about 2 medium bananas)

¼ c. olive oil

1/2 t. vanilla

1 c. whole wheat flour

2 T. flax meal

1 t. baking powder

1 t. baking soda

1 t. cinnamon

1/4 t. salt

1/4 c. packed brown sugar

1/2 c. chopped walnuts

2 T. sugar (optional)

Preheat oven to 400 degrees. Heat blueberries in microwave on high with 1 tablespoon water for 30 seconds or until thawed. Let cool. Mix wet ingredients together, except for blueberries. Mix dry ingredients together and add to wet mixture. Mix until just until moistened. Fold in the blueberries and walnuts. Place muffin liners in pan, or spray muffin tin with nonstick spray. Fill liners half full and sprinkle tops with small amount of sugar. Bake muffins for 22 minutes, or until a toothpick comes out clean.

13

Mini Banana Sandwiches

Makes 1 serving

1 banana, peeled

1 to 2 T. honey

1 to 2 T. peanut butter

1/3 c. wheat germ or flax meal

Cut the banana into 1/2-inch slices. Spread a small amount of peanut butter on each slice, sprinkle with 1 teaspoon of wheat germ or flax meal, and a drizzle of honey. Place second banana slice on top. Serve with a toothpick for less messy eating if needed.

TIP: This is a great recipe for your kids to practice their cooking skills! Cut of the top of the banana, and let them peel it, then have them slice the banana with a butter knife. They can assemble the sandwiches, too; it gets messy, but it's also a lot of fun!

Egg Rollup with Salsa and Guacamole

2 servings

1 small whole wheat tortilla

1 egg

1 T. milk

guacamole (page 81)

pantry salsa (page 88)

Spray a small skillet with cooking spray. Stir the egg and milk together in a bowl. Pour egg mixture into the skillet and cook 2 minutes, turning halfway through. Spread the tortilla with guacamole, and lay the egg over top. Roll up and secure with a toothpick. Serve with salsa for dipping.

(To save time and dishes, cook the egg and milk in a microwave safe bowl sprayed with cooking spray for 1 minute. Break up the cooked egg with a fork and roll up in the tortilla as above.)

16

Apricot Pitas

Makes 2 servings

4 apricots, seeded and cubed

2 pita bread pieces (4 halves)

1 c. cottage cheese

12 thin slices of cucumber or
red bell pepper

2 T. sunflower seeds

Fill each pita with cottage cheese, apricots, and cucumber, then sprinkle each half with 1/4 of the sunflower seeds.

TIP: Kids have to learn food prep skills in order to help in the kitchen. If they're very young or new to helping, have them start by putting their hand over yours while you're slicing vegetables. As they get more experienced, have them hold the knife while you put your hand over to help. Before long, they'll be making their own snacks and maybe even helping with dinner!

Breakfast Splits

Makes 1 serving

1 small banana

1/2 c. plain or vanilla yogurt

1/4 c. granola or high fiber cereal

1/2 c. sliced or chopped fresh fruit

Peel banana and cut in half lengthwise and place in shallow bowl. Top with yogurt, cereal and fruit.

TIP: Fiber is important to a child's diet: it keeps them full and helps with digestion. Many kids do not get enough fiber. Boost your child's fiber intake by choosing a cereal with at least 5 grams of fiber per serving.

QUICK AND EASY SNACK IDEAS FOR FOCUS

GREEK YOGURT WITH FRUIT

HIGH FIBER CEREAL WITH MILK

WHOLE WHEAT BAGEL WITH PEANUT BUTTER

FRESH OR CANNED PEARS WITH COTTAGE CHEESE

CUBES OF CHEESE WITH SLICED FRESH FRUIT

HARD BOILED EGG WITH SLICED VEGGIES

A HANDFUL OF ALMONDS

SUPER
SNACKS FOR
AFTER SCHOOL

After school, super kids need something quick and filling to keep them playing till dinner time.

Apple Dippers

Makes 2 servings

2 T. peanut butter

2 small apples

2 T. honey

1/4 c. wheat germ or flax meal

about 2 T. fruit juice

In a small microwaveable bowl, melt peanut butter for approximately 15 seconds on high. Add honey and fruit juice as needed to thin to dipping consistency. Slice apples into wedges. Place wheat germ or flax meal in small bowl, let kids dip the apple slices into the honey-peanut butter sauce, then into the wheat germ or flax meal.

Fruity Oatmeal

Makes 2 servings

1 c. 100% fruit juice

1 c. water

1 apple, diced

1/4 c. dried fruit

1 c. old-fashioned oats

1/4 t. cinnamon

dash of salt

1/4 c. chopped walnuts

In large microwaveable bowl, mix all ingredients except walnuts. Cook on high in microwave for 2 minutes, or until thick. Divide into 2 bowls and top with walnuts.

TIP: When buying fruit juice make sure you see 100% juice on the label to avoid added sugar.

Quick Quesadilla with Easy Applesauce

Makes 2 servings

1 whole wheat tortilla

1/2 c. shredded cheese

1 c. Easy Applesauce (page 86)
or 1 c. unsweetened applesauce mixed
with 1/2 t. of cinnamon

Place cheese on half of tortilla, fold over, and microwave for 30-60 seconds until cheese is melted. Cut into 8 wedges with a pizza cutter. Serve with Easy Applesauce for dipping.

Little Pizzas

Makes 2 servings

1 whole wheat bagel or whole wheat
English muffin

4 cherry or grape tomatoes

2 T. marinara or pizza sauce

1/2 c. shredded cheese

Preheat oven or toaster oven to 350 degrees. Slice bagel in half. Slice tomatoes thinly and place on bagel. Spread 1 tablespoon sauce over the tomatoes. If your kids are extra picky about tomato chunks, chop finely and mix with marinara sauce before spreading. Top with cheese. Bake for 8 minutes, or until cheese is melted.

TIP: Let your child help with spreading on the sauce, topping with tomatoes, and sprinkling the cheese on top.

Tomato Wraps

Makes 2 servings

1/3 c. vegetable cream cheese or hummus (page 82)

6 spinach leaves

1 tomato, sliced into thin rounds

2 whole wheat tortillas

Spread a bit of cream cheese or hummus on each tortilla. Place 3 slices of tomato on each tortilla, then top each with a spinach leaf. Roll up the tortilla and cut into 6 rounds. Secure each round with a toothpick as needed.

Cucumber Boats

Makes 4 servings

2 celery stalks

1 large carrot or 5 baby carrots

1/4 c. cottage cheese

1 large cucumber

2 T. ranch dressing

1/4 c. sunflower seeds (optional)

Peel cucumber, slice lengthwise, and remove the seeds. Divide each cucumber half into 2 boats. Finely chop celery and carrots and place in a bowl. Stir in cottage cheese, and ranch dressing. Spread mixture into cucumber cavity, sprinkle sunflower seeds over the top and serve.

TIP: If your child isn't fond of celery and carrots, you could substitute any chopped vegetable of their choice.

Creamy Fruit Salad

Makes 4 servings

1/4 c. vanilla or plain yogurt

1 T. honey (optional if using vanilla yogurt)

1/4 c. chopped almonds or walnuts

1 apple, chopped

1 banana, sliced

2 kiwis, peeled and sliced

1/2 c. seedless grapes, halved

Stir honey and yogurt until smooth. Combine nuts, chopped apple, banana slices, kiwi slices, and halved grapes. Add yogurt mixture, stir to coat, and chill until ready to serve.

TIP: Yogurt can be a healthy choice, but it can also be packed with sugar and other artificial stuff. Every teaspoon of sugar is 4 grams, and many varieties of yogurt can have 20 grams or more of sugar per serving! Avoid this added sugar by buying unsweetened ("plain") yogurt in bulk, and adding in sugar, honey, or jam to taste. You'll probably use much less than 5 teaspoon's worth! You can also decrease sugar by mixing plain yogurt with vanilla yogurt, adding more plain as you get used to the taste.

Kohlrabi Rounds

Serves 1

1 small kohlrabi

1/4 c. Extra Special Egg Salad (page 84)

Peel kohlrabi and slice into 1/4 inch slices. Top each slice with 1 teaspoon egg salad.

You can substitute chicken or tuna salad, depending on preference — see chicken salad recipe on page 92.

TIP: Kohlrabi is a super food that is packed with antioxidants! It is in the same family as broccoli, but it has a more mild flavor and many kids love it!

Cracker Stackers

Makes 1 serving

8 whole grain crackers

1 small piece of fruit (apple, pear, plum, or peach)

1 oz. cheese (cheddar, pepperjack, mozzarella, or muenster)

Slice fruit into 8 wedges. Slice cheese into 8 pieces. Top each cracker with one slice of cheese and one wedge of fruit.

TIP: Let your kids get creative and try different combinations of their favorite cheeses and fruits. Put out a plate of a variety of choices and see what cracker stacker creations they come up with. This is a simple way to expose them to new flavors and be adventurous with trying new foods.

QUICK AND EASY SNACK IDEAS FOR AFTER SCHOOL

VEGGIES AND DIP

FRUIT WITH PEANUT BUTTER

REGULAR INSTANT OATMEAL WITH FRUIT

COTTAGE CHEESE WITH PEACHES

TURKEY AND CHEESE ROLLED INTO A

WHOLE GRAIN TORTILLA

SUPER
SNACKS FOR
PLAY

· ·

Before sporting events, give your super kid the quick energy they need — carbohydrates and a little protein without too much fiber or fat.

Easy Fruit Pocket Pies

Makes 6 servings

12 slices whole wheat bread

6 T. Easy Applesauce (page 86) or unsweetened applesauce

3/4 c. fresh berries

2 T. canola oil

2 T. sugar

1/2 t. cinnamon

Preheat oven to 350 degrees. Spoon 1 tablespoon of applesauce in the center of each of 6 bread slices. Top each with a few berries and then a second slice of bread. Lightly press the edges of the top slice of bread around the filling. Trim the crusts from each pie. Use a sandwich crimper or fork to crimp the edges and seal in the fruit. Brush tops of each pie with a small amount of oil. Place on a lightly greased baking sheet. Mix together sugar and cinnamon, and sprinkle each pie with cinnamon-sugar mixture. Bake for 18-20 minutes, until lightly toasted. Cool completely before serving.

TIP: Choose a bread with 2 or more grams of fiber per slice

Quick Strawberry-Rhubarb "Pie" for One

Makes 1 serving

1/4 c. strawberries, sliced

1/4 c. rhubarb, sliced

1/4 c. vanilla yogurt

1/4 c. crushed graham crackers

Combine strawberries and rhubarb in a small microwaveable bowl. Heat on high in the microwave for 45 seconds or until bubbling. Remove from microwave and chill in freezer at least 5 minutes or up to 1 hour. Top with yogurt and crushed graham crackers.

TIP: This is a great recipe to make in the spring, when strawberries and rhubarb are in season. Have your kids help harvest some from your garden, or let them have their pick at your local farmer's market. If you have extra fruit, chop and freeze it for later use.

Energy Bites

Makes 12 servings

1 c. old-fashioned oats

1 c. toasted coconut flakes

1/2 c. chocolate chips

1/2 c. peanut butter

1/2 c. flax meal or wheat germ

1/3 c. honey

1 t. vanilla

In a medium bowl, mix all ingredients until well combined. Chill for at least 30 minutes. Roll dough into about 24 one-inch balls. Store in an airtight container in the refrigerator.

TIP: Flax meal is ground flaxseeds (which are not easily digested whole) — they are high in healthy fats and protein along with fiber.

Apple Oat Bars

Makes 16 bars

Base:

1-1/2 c. whole wheat flour

3/4 c. old-fashioned oats

1 t. baking powder

1/2 t. salt

1/2 c. packed brown sugar

2 T. canola or olive oil

1/2 c. Easy Applesauce (page 86) or unsweetened applesauce

1 egg

1 t. vanilla extract

Filling:

1 c. Easy Applesauce (page 86) or unsweetened applesauce

1/2 c. raisins

1 t. cinnamon

Preheat oven to 375 degrees. Coat an 8 x 8 inch baking pan with non-stick spray and set aside. For the base, in a medium bowl, combine flour, oats, baking powder, and salt. In a large bowl, mix the brown sugar with the oil until well blended. Add applesauce, egg, and vanilla. Add dry mixture into applesauce mixture and stir well. Spread half of the base into the pan. For the filling, combine applesauce, raisins, cinnamon, and brown sugar in a small bowl. Spread this mixture over top of base. Spoon the remaining half of the base over top of the filling. Bake until lightly brown, 30-35 minutes. Cool for at least 15 minutes before cutting into bars.

Quick Baked Apples

Makes 4 servings

2 tart apples, medium-sized

1 T. packed brown sugar

1/2 t. cinnamon

1/4 c. old-fashioned oats

1/4 c. dried fruit or chopped nuts

1 c. vanilla yogurt

Cut apples in half lengthwise and remove cores with a spoon. In a microwaveable dish, place apple halves cut side up. Combine brown sugar, cinnamon, oats, and fruit or nuts in a small bowl. Top each apple half with 1/4 of the mixture. Cover dish, and microwave 3 to 3-1/2 minutes, until soft. Let cool. Serve with 1/4 cup yogurt over top of each apple half.

Watermelon Berry Sorbet

Makes 4 servings

1 c. water

1/3 c. honey

2 c. seedless watermelon, cubed

2 c. strawberries, hulled

1 T. mint, minced (optional)

Bring water and honey to a boil. Cook, stirring continuously, until honey is well dissolved. Set aside to cool. Place the watermelon and strawberries in a blender. Add honey mixture. Cover and blend until smooth, about 2-3 minutes. Transfer mixture to a 9 X 13 inch baking dish. Freeze 1 hour, until slightly firm around the edges. Stir in mint and freeze until firm, about 2 hours. When ready to serve, transfer mixture to a blender, and process for 2 minutes, until smooth.

TIP: If fresh strawberries are not available, frozen fruit works just as well. When you add the warm honey mixture, the fruit will thaw just enough to make blending easier.

Smart Cookies

Makes 24 cookies

3 bananas, mashed

1/2 c. Easy Applesauce (page 86) or unsweetened applesauce

2 c. uncooked quick cooking oats

1/4 c. milk

2 t. vanilla

1 t. cinnamon

1 T. brown sugar

1/2 c. dried fruit
(cranberries, blueberries, or raisins)

1/2 c. crushed walnuts

1/2 c. mini chocolate chips

Preheat oven to 350 degrees. Mix first 4 ingredients by hand and let sit 5 minutes. Add remaining ingredients and blend with an electric mixer for 2 minutes to combine. Heap dough by teaspoonful onto a greased baking sheet, and flatten with the back of the spoon. Bake 15-20 minutes until lightly browned. Cool completely and store in an airtight container.

Red and White Fruit Salad

Makes 2 serving

1 T. honey

1 T. lime juice (about 1/2 of a fresh lime)

1 pomegranate, chilled

1 banana

Combine honey and lime juice in a small bowl. Seed the pomegranates. Divide seeds between two plates. Cut bananas into 1/2 inch slices and arrange around the pomegranate seeds. Drizzle with honey-lime dressing.

TIP: Cut pomegranate in half and use your fingers to scoop out the seeds and separate them from the center of the fruit. To save time you may find fresh or frozen pomegranates seeds in your grocery store.

Pumpkin Muffins

Makes 12 servings

1-1/2 c. whole wheat flour

1 t. baking powder

1 t. cinnamon

1/4 t. nutmeg

1/4 t. baking soda

1/3 c. canola or olive oil

1 c. pumpkin puree

1/2 c. plain yogurt

1 egg and 1 egg white

1/2 c. packed brown sugar

1/2 c. chopped walnuts

1 T. sugar

Preheat oven to 350 degrees. Place muffin papers in tin, or spray with nonstick spray. Mix flour, baking powder, cinnamon, nutmeg, and baking soda in a small bowl. In a large bowl, mix oil, pumpkin, yogurt, eggs, and sugar until combined. Add flour mixture to pumpkin mixture and stir just until well moistened. Divide batter into muffin tin. Sprinkle walnuts and sugar over the top of each muffin. Bake 35 minutes, until tops are browned.

TIP: If you have leftover pumpkin from a recipe, pack it in an ice cube tray and freeze it for later use in recipes, or to add to pancake batter or smoothies.

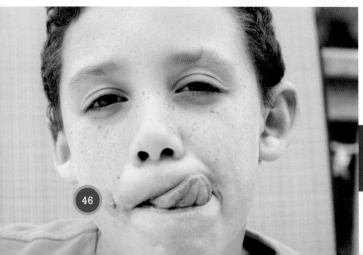

QUICK AND EASY SNACK IDEAS FOR PLAY

LOW FAT GRANOLA BAR

WHOLE WHEAT TOAST WITH JAM OR HONEY

BOWL OF CEREAL WITH SKIM MILK

LOW FAT YOGURT

SLICES OF FRUIT

SUPER SNACKS FOR AFTER PLAY

After sports and playing outside, kids need some protein and good hydration to replenish what they've burned off.

TIP: Smoothies are a great way to get in lots of healthy fruits and vegetables, especially for kids who are finicky. Bananas are a nice base for smoothies — they provide a sweet flavor and smooth texture. Spinach is a good addition to smoothies — it doesn't have much flavor when mixed with other ingredients, but is packed with nutrients and adds a bright green color. Use plain yogurt if possible — if the smoothie needs a little sweetener, try honey, add some 100% fruit juice, or use vanilla yogurt. Keep frozen fruit on hand to mix into smoothies — berries are great, but you can also add peaches, mango, pineapple, or any other fruit your child prefers. Make up your own names for your smoothies (Sophia's strawberry surprise), or color coordinate for a holiday (spinach green St. Patrick's day smoothies), or for a sports team (beet red Badgers smoothies).

Fruit and Vegetable Smoothies

Makes 2 servings

Berry Beet Smoothie

1/2 c. vanilla yogurt

1 banana

1/2 c. fresh or frozen strawberries

1/4 c. cooked beets

Banana Orange Delight

1/4 c. plain yogurt

1/2 c. orange juice

1 banana

1/2 c. cooked carrots

Green Slime

1/2 c. plain yogurt

1/2 c. fresh or frozen strawberries

1 banana

1 c. spinach leaves, packed

Place all ingredients in a blender and process until smooth, stopping blender to scrape down sides as needed. Serve immediately or chill. The mixture can also be frozen into popsicles.

Blueberry Breakfast Bars

Makes 12 servings

2-1/2 c. crushed high fiber cereal

3 T. honey

1 c. plain greek yogurt

1 c. blueberry or vanilla greek yogurt

1 c. frozen blueberries

2/3 c. nonfat dry milk

Spray 8 x 8 inch baking pan with nonstick spray. In a blender or food processor, mix honey, yogurt, fruit, and nonfat milk until well blended. Fold 1 cup of cereal into yogurt mix. Pour 3/4 cup cereal evenly into pan. Spread yogurt mix over top of cereal in pan. Top with remaining cereal. Freeze for a minimum of 4 hours or until firm. Cut into bars and store in the freezer until ready to serve.

TIP: When choosing a cereal, look for one with at least 5 grams of fiber and protein per serving. For bonus points, choose a cereal with less than 10 grams (2 teaspoons) of sugar per serving.

Fruit Kabobs with Yogurt Dip

Makes 6 servings

2 c. of fruit of your choice
(apple, strawberries, clementines,
banana, kiwi, or grapes)

1 - 8 oz. can chunk pineapple

1 c. vanilla yogurt

1 T. lemon or lime juice

Peel fruit if needed and cut into bite sized chunks. Drain pineapple and reserve juice. Dip fruits that turn brown after peeling (bananas and apples) into reserved pineapple juice. Thread fruit pieces onto skewers or toothpicks. Stir together yogurt and lemon juice until smooth. Refrigerate until ready to serve.

TIP: Serving fruits and vegetables with healthy dips is a good way to encourage kids to try new foods.

Banana-Strawberry Freezies

Makes 4 servings

1 c. vanilla yogurt

1 c. frozen strawberries

1 banana

Process all ingredients in a food processor or blender until smooth. Pour mixture into popsicle molds or single serving bowls. Freeze overnight. Use warm water to unmold.

Carrot Lemonade

Makes 6 servings

1 lb. carrots, peeled and cut into chunks

2 c. water

3 c. pineapple or unsweetened
white grape juice

3/4 c. lemon juice

additional water if needed

Combine carrots and water in a saucepan
and bring to boil. Reduce heat to a simmer
and cover for 30 minutes or until soft. Cool
slightly and transfer carrots and water to
a blender. Add 1 cup of juice, cover and blend
until smooth. Transfer the blended mixture
to a pitcher and stir in remaining juice and
lemon juice. Serve cold or over ice.

Veggie Wraps

Makes 4 servings

2 small whole wheat tortillas

1 c. hummus (page 82)

1 bell pepper (red, green or yellow), seeded

1 large or 5 baby carrots

1/2 large cucumber

Chop all vegetables. Spread hummus on tortillas. Spread chopped vegetables evenly over the top of the hummus. Roll up each tortilla and slice into 2 halves.

TIP: Hummus is made from garbanzo beans (chickpeas), and is packed with fiber and protein. You can make your own if you have the time, or find some in the refrigerated section of your grocery store.

Rainbow Winter Fruit Salad

Makes 4 servings

1/2 c. pomegranate seeds

1/2 c. mandarin oranges

2 kiwis

1 c. blueberries

1/2 c. chunk pineapple

1/2 c. lime or vanilla yogurt

slivered almonds (optional)

Wash, drain and rinse mandarin oranges. Peel kiwis and slice into chunks. Wash blueberries. Starting with pomegranate seeds, layer 1/4 of each fruit in individual glasses or serving bowls. Just before serving top with yogurt and sprinkle with almonds if desired.

TIP: Let your child help you identify each fruit and its color, and decide in which order the fruit should be layered.

Trail Mix

Makes 4 servings

1 c. from each category

Category 1: Cereal

mini shredded wheat

oat squares

granola

Category 2: Dried Fruit

dried cranberries

raisins

dried blueberries

Category 3: Nuts

almonds

walnuts

soynuts

Category 4: Sweet

dark or semi-sweet chocolate chips

candy-coated chocolate pieces

carob chips

Mix together and store in
an airtight canister.

Open-Faced Banana Sandwiches

Makes 2 servings

1 slice whole grain bread

2 T. peanut butter

1 banana

1/2 c. raisins

Spread peanut butter on bread. Place banana slices on bread and sprinkle raisins over top. Cut into 4 pieces and serve.

TIP: Let your child create a design on the bread with the banana slices and raisins.

QUICK AND EASY SNACKS FOR AFTER PLAY

BOTTLE OF WATER TO REHYDRATE **PLUS**

STRING CHEESE

YOGURT

TRAIL MIX

FRESH FRUIT

POPCORN

HIGH FIBER CRACKERS

SUPER
SNACKS FOR
A CROWD

Snacks for a crowd are easily multiplied
and appeal to a wide range of tastes.

Fruit Pizza

Makes 8 servings

1 large egg white

1/4 c. canola or olive oil

1/4 c. packed brown sugar

1/3 c. whole wheat flour

1/4 t. ground cinnamon

1/4 t. baking soda

1 c. uncooked quick cooking oats

3 oz. cream cheese, softened

1/3 c. vanilla yogurt

Sliced fruit and berries

Preheat oven to 375 degrees. Beat egg white in a medium bowl until foamy. Add oil and sugar, and beat until smooth. In a small bowl, mix flour, cinnamon, baking soda, and oats; add to sugar mixture. Line a baking sheet with aluminum foil and spray with cooking spray. Spread the dough into a 9-inch circle. Bake 12 minutes until lightly browned. Remove from oven and let cool. In a small bowl, mix together cream cheese and yogurt until smooth; chill. Transfer the cooled crust to a serving plate. Spread yogurt mixture over crust. Arrange sliced fruit on top. Cover and refrigerate until just before serving. Cut into 8 slices and serve.

Strawberry Oatmeal Rhubarb Bread

Makes 12 servings

1 c. whole wheat flour

1/4 c. brown sugar

3 t. baking powder

1/2 t. salt

1/4 t. cinnamon

1 c. old-fashioned oats

1 egg, lightly beaten

1 c. milk

2 T. canola or olive oil

1 c. chopped rhubarb

1 c. chopped strawberries

Preheat oven to 425°F. In a large bowl mix flour, brown sugar, baking powder, salt, and cinnamon. Stir in oats. Add egg, milk, and oil; stir gently until just combined. Fold in rhubarb and strawberries. Pour into a greased loaf pan and bake 30 minutes.

Squash Bread

Makes 10 servings

1-1/2 c. whole wheat flour

2 t. cinnamon

1 t. baking powder

1/2 t. baking soda

2 eggs

1/2 c. brown sugar

1/2 c. canola oil

2 t. vanilla extract

2 c. grated zucchini or summer squash

Heat oven to 350 degrees. Mix dry ingredients together. Beat eggs, sugar, oil and vanilla until well blended. Squeeze the squash with paper towels to remove some of the moisture, then fold into egg mixture. Add dry ingredients and mix only until moist. Spray a loaf pan with cooking spray. Pour batter into prepared pan and bake 40 minutes, until a toothpick comes out clean. Cool completely and serve.

TIP: Teach your child early how to crack eggs. Start by having them hold your hand while you crack eggs into a bowl. When they ask to do it themselves, give them a bowl and an egg, and hold their hand while they do it the first few times. It will take many tries and a little bit of a mess before they can do it without getting shells in the bowl, but they will be very proud to learn this skill.

Summer Bounty Salad

Makes 12 servings

7 c. of cut-up fresh vegetables (zucchini, broccoli, carrots, radishes, cauliflower, kohlrabi, sugar snap peas, green beans — anything in season!)

1 bell pepper

2 tomatoes

2/3 c. salad dressing of your choice

Wash and cut vegetables into 1/2 inch chunks. If desired, seed tomatoes before slicing. Combine all vegetables with dressing, stir to coat well. Cover and chill 1-3 hours before serving.

TIP: This recipe can be entirely adapted to your child's preference — let them choose their favorite vegetables, and use whatever dressing they prefer.

Canned Fruit Salad

Makes 8 servings

1 (large-15 oz.) can mandarin oranges

1 can tropical fruit mix

1 can pineapple tidbits

4 oz. plain greek yogurt

4 oz. flavored yogurt (peach, key lime, or vanilla are all great)

1/2 c. chopped walnuts

Drain & rinse all fruit and put it in a large bowl. Add greek yogurt and flavored yogurt. Mix with fruit. Top with chopped nuts. Refrigerate until serving.

TIP: If you can't find a canned fruit in 100% juice, try to buy one that's packed in "light syrup," then drain and rinse well before using.

Caramel Popcorn

Makes 8 servings

6 c. popped popcorn

1/2 c. peanuts (optional)

1/2 c. sunflower seeds (optional)

1 T. molasses

1 T. maple syrup

1/3 c. honey

Preheat oven to 350 degrees. Place popcorn, peanuts, and sunflower seeds in a large bowl. In a small bowl, combine molasses, maple syrup, and honey; stir until well blended. Pour over popcorn and toss until well coated. Spread onto a greased baking sheet and bake for 15 minutes. Let cool completely before transferring to an airtight container for storage. Alternately, form the coated popcorn into balls before baking.

TIP: What is the best sweetener to use?

Most sweeteners (honey, sugar, brown sugar, molasses, maple syrup) have the same number of calories for the amount of sweetness they provide in a recipe, so they're all the same from that perspective. Honey and molasses add moisture to recipes, and may also have some health benefits. Brown sugar also adds some moisture along with a depth to the flavor of recipes, but has no other health benefits. Most of the recipes in this book call for brown sugar or honey, but it's really a personal preference. If you prefer another sweetener, just be sure to use the minimum amount needed to have the recipe suit your taste buds!

Layer Dip

Makes 8 servings

1/4 c. sour cream

1/4 c. plain yogurt

1 can black beans, rinsed

1 avocado

1 lime

pinch of salt and pepper

1 c. shredded cheddar cheese

1/2 c. tomato, chopped

1 T. green onion, chopped (optional)

Mix sour cream and yogurt; spread across bottom of a glass bowl or 9-inch pie plate. Sprinkle black beans across sour cream mixture. Mash together avocado with lime, salt, and pepper; spread across black bean layer. Add a layer of cheese, then top with tomato and green onion. Serve with pita or tortilla chips (pages 72-73).

TIP: Avocados are ripe when the skin gives just a little bit when you press on it. If there are only firm avocados available, let them sit in the fruit bowl for a couple of days until they are ready.

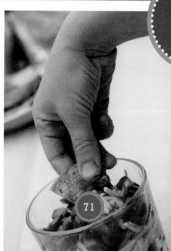

Pita Chips

Makes 8 servings

8 whole wheat pita pockets

2 T. olive oil

1 T. garlic powder

1 t. salt

1 t. garlic salt

Preheat oven to 350 degrees. Split pita pockets in half. Brush one side of each pita pocket with olive oil. Mix together garlic powder, salt, and garlic salt. Sprinkle each pita pocket with salt mixture. Cut each into 4 triangles. Bake 15-20 minutes, until light brown.

Sweet Potato Chips

Makes 8 servings

2 medium sweet potatoes

1 T. olive oil

1/2 t. salt

Preheat oven to 400 degrees. Wash sweet potatoes. Slice into 1/8 inch rounds. Toss with olive oil and spread in single layer on 2 baking sheets. Sprinkle with salt. Bake 22-25 minutes, flipping halfway through, until edges are crisp.

Tortilla Chips

Makes 8 servings

1 package corn tortillas

1 T. canola oil

3 T. lime juice

1 t. garlic salt

1 t. chili powder

Preheat oven to 350 degrees. Mix oil and lime juice. Brush each tortilla with the oil mixture. Cut each tortilla into 8 wedges and arrange onto a lightly oiled baking sheet. Sprinkle with salt and chili powder. Bake 7 minutes, rotate the pan, and bake another 7-8 minutes, until crisp and very lightly browned.

Kale Chips

Makes 8 servings

1 bunch kale

1 T. olive oil

a sprinkle of seasoned salt

Preheat oven to 350 degrees. Line a baking sheet with parchment paper. Cut stems from kale, and tear leaves into 1 inch pieces. Wash and dry kale. In a large bowl, toss kale with olive oil and sprinkle with seasoning salt. Bake 10-15 minutes, until edges are brown.

Cranberry Oatmeal Snack Bars

Makes 24 servings

1 c. dried cranberries

1/4 c. 100% fruit juice

1/2 c. packed brown sugar

2/3 c. olive or canola oil

2 eggs

1/4 t. salt

1-1/2 c. whole wheat flour

1-1/2 c. old-fashioned oats

1 t. baking powder

1/4 c. chopped nuts

Preheat oven to 350 degrees. Spray a 9 x 13 inch pan with cooking spray. In a microwave safe bowl, combine juice and cranberries. Microwave on high for 10 seconds and let cool. Beat together brown sugar and oil until fluffy. Add eggs one at a time and mix well. Combine the dry ingredients and add to the sugar mixture. Add cranberries and nuts and fold together. Spread evenly into the prepared pan. Bake 20-22 minutes or until set.

QUICK AND EASY SNACK
IDEAS FOR A CROWD

WHOLE GRAIN CHIPS WITH SALSA OR GUACAMOLE

CHEESE AND FRUIT WITH WHOLE GRAIN CRACKERS

VEGGIES WITH HUMMUS OR DIP

FRESH FRUIT

POPCORN

SUPER STAPLES

· ·

Staples are the building blocks
for healthy snacking habits.

Maple Nut Granola

Makes 12 servings

4 c. old-fashioned oats

1 c. walnut pieces

1/4 c. packed brown sugar

1 t. salt

1/2 t. cinnamon

1/2 t. nutmeg

3/4 c. pure maple syrup

1/2 c. olive oil

1 c. dried cranberries

Heat oven to 300. Combine oats, walnuts, brown sugar, sea salt, cinnamon, and nutmeg in a large bowl. Add maple syrup and olive oil and stir until all ingredients are well mixed. Spread mixture into a baking sheet and bake 45 minutes, stirring every 10 minutes. Let cool slightly and stir in cranberries. Store in an airtight container.

TIP: Granola can be stored for up to a week in an air tight container. It also freezes very well to use later.

Omega-3 Granola

Makes 10 servings

2 c. old–fashioned oats

1 c. coarsely chopped almonds

1/2 c. coconut flakes

1/2 c. shelled sunflower seeds

1/4 c. flax meal

1/4 c. wheat germ

1/2 c. honey

2 T. canola oil

Heat oven to 300. Mix dry ingredients together. Stir together honey and oil in small bowl then stir into oat mixture. Spread evenly on a well greased baking sheet. Bake for 30-35 minutes, stirring halfway through. Cool completely and store in an airtight container.

TIP: When making granola and other baked goods, have your child help you identify ingredients and measure them out.

Guacamole Dip

Makes 4 servings

1 large ripe avocado

1 T. lime juice (about 1/2 of a fresh lime)

1 small tomato or 4 grape tomatoes, diced

Dash of ground pepper

Dash of garlic salt

1 small onion, minced (optional)

Cut the avocado in half around the pit, twist both halves in opposite directions and remove pit. Scoop out flesh into a medium bowl. Mash the avocado and add remaining ingredients. Stir until well combined. Serve with vegetables, pita, or tortilla chips (pages 72-73).

TIP: Your kids will love to help with this recipe. Have them twist open the avocados after you have cut them, and then they can scoop or squeeze out the avocado halves. Show them how to squeeze the lime, and give them a chance to try. Then give them a fork to mash the avocado and stir in the tomatoes. You may need to assist a bit, but they will be so proud to have helped!

Hummus

Makes 6 servings

1 16 oz. can of garbanzo beans (chickpeas)

juice of 1 lemon

2 T. tahini, which is sesame seed paste
(or if omitting, add 1 extra T. of olive oil)

1 T. olive oil

1 clove of garlic

1/4 t. garlic salt

dash of pepper

Drain and rinse garbanzo beans. Add beans and remaining ingredients to the bowl of a food processor or blender. Process until smooth and creamy. Keep refrigerated until time to serve.

Spinach Dip

Makes 4 servings

2 c. fresh spinach

1 c. plain greek yogurt

1/4 c. green onions, including tops

pinch of salt

dash of pepper

dash of onion powder

Place spinach in a food processor or blender until finely chopped. Scoop out spinach into a paper towel, and squeeze out excess moisture. Return to processor or blender and add remaining ingredients, process until well blended. Chill and serve with fresh vegetables or pita chips (page 72).

83

Extra Special Egg Salad

Makes 4 servings

4 hardboiled eggs

1/4 c. plain greek yogurt

1 avocado

pinch of salt

pinch of black pepper

1 stalk celery, chopped (optional)

1 c. spinach, chopped (optional)

Peel eggs. In a large bowl, mash eggs with yogurt and avocado. Season with salt and pepper, and stir to blend. Add celery and spinach, if desired. Chill and serve.

TIP: Fat is not bad for you! Kids especially need lots of good quality fat to feed their growing brains and nervous systems. It also keeps blood sugar more even and takes longer to digest, keeping you feeling full. In general, the best sources of fat are plant sources — nuts and seeds, plant oils, and avocado are great options.

Colorful Bean Dip

Makes 12 servings

1 can black beans

1 can pinto beans

1 c. frozen corn, thawed

4 green onions, chopped

2 c. tomatoes, chopped

1 red pepper, seeded and chopped

1 jalapeño pepper (optional),
seeded and chopped

1 bunch cilantro, finely chopped

1 c. Italian dressing

Drain and rinse beans and combine with corn. Stir all remaining vegetables to bean and corn mixture. Add Italian dressing and mix well. Chill for at least 30 minutes prior to serving. Serve with tortilla chips (page 73).

85

Easy Applesauce

Makes 4 servings, about 2 cups

2 lbs. apples

1/2 c. water

cinnamon to taste (optional)

Core and slice apples. Place apples and 1/2 cup water in a large saucepan. Simmer covered over medium heat until apples are very tender. Remove from heat and mash with an immersion blender or transfer to a blender to process. Return to heat and simmer uncovered for 5 minutes, stirring frequently. Add cinnamon.

Apple Chips

Makes 2 servings

2 apples

1 t. cinnamon

Preheat oven to 275 degrees. Core apples and slice 1/8 inch thick into rounds. Line a baking sheet with foil and spray with non-stick cooking spray. Place apples on baking sheet and sprinkle cinnamon evenly over apples. Bake for 1 hour, flip slices, and bake for another hour. Let cool, and store in an airtight container

Asian Peanut Dip

Makes 1 cup

1/2 c. natural style peanut butter

1/3 c. reduced fat firm silken tofu

3 T. packed brown sugar

juice from half of a lime (about 2 T.)

2 T. soy sauce

1/2 t. crushed red pepper

2 garlic cloves, crushed

Process all ingredients in a blender or food processor until smooth.

TIP: Tofu is made from soybeans and is very high in protein. It doesn't have much flavor on its own, and it blends into recipes very well.

Pantry Salsa

Makes 3 cups

2 14 oz. cans diced tomatoes

1 4 oz. can green chiles

1/2 small onion, peeled

1 clove garlic, peeled and smashed

1 jalapeño pepper (optional), seeded

1 t. honey

1/4 t. salt

1/4 t. ground cumin

2 T. cilantro (if in season)

juice of 1 lime

Drain tomatoes and chiles and place in food processor or blender. Add remaining ingredients. Pulse for 30-60 seconds until ingredients are finely chopped and well mixed. Store in refrigerator until ready to serve.

Roasted Tomato Salsa

Makes 2 cups

6 Roma tomatoes

1/4 red onion

1 jalapeño pepper (optional)

1 clove of garlic

1 T. white vinegar

pinch of salt

1 T. chopped cilantro

Heat oven to 350 degrees. Line a baking sheet with foil and roast tomatoes, whole, for 15-20 minutes on the center rack of the oven. Let cool slightly, then place in a food processor or blender with remaining ingredients and process until well combined. Refrigerate until ready to serve.

TIP: Many kids are picky about spice in their foods — they have a more sensitive palate and may perceive even a bit of black pepper as being "too spicy." If your kid likes a bit of heat in their food, feel free to add more hot peppers to suit their palate.

Fruit Salsa

Makes 2 cups

4 ripe but firm peaches, pitted

2-3 T. chopped shallots or onions

2 jalapeño peppers (optional), seeded and chopped

juice of a lemon

2 T. chopped fresh mint

1 t. ground ginger

pinch of salt

pinch of ground pepper

Put the peaches, shallots, and jalapeños in a food processor. Pulse to chop coarsely. Add remaining ingredients and pulse another 2-3 times, just until well combined. Do not over-process. Chill until serving, at least 1 hour if possible. Serve with tortilla chips (page 73).

Basic Veggie Dip

Makes 4 servings

1 c. plain greek yogurt

1/2 T. chopped fresh dill (or 1 t. dried)

1/2 T. chopped fresh chives

1 T. chopped green onions

dash of salt

dash of pepper

Mix all ingredients, chill for at least 1 hour before serving.

TIP: This basic dip can be adjusted to your family's taste by adding any fresh or dried herbs of your choice.

Chicken Salad

Makes 6 servings

3/4 c. plain greek yogurt

2 T. mayonnaise

2 t. Dijon mustard

1 lb. cooked chicken, roughly chopped

1 c. frozen peas, thawed

1/2 c. dried cranberries

1/4 c. slivered almonds

Stir together plain greek yogurt, mayonnaise, and mustard in a large bowl. Add chicken and peas, and mix well. Chill for at least 30 minutes. Just before serving, stir in cranberries and almonds and mix well.

SUPER STAPLES

OLD-FASHIONED OATS

PLAIN GREEK YOGURT

WHOLE WHEAT FLOUR

NATURAL PEANUT BUTTER

FLAX MEAL OR WHEAT GERM

CHOPPED NUTS

DRIED FRUIT

CINNAMON

HONEY

EGGS

Food Allergies

Allergies and sensitivities to foods have become very common, affecting up to 10 percent of kids. The most common allergy foods are peanuts, tree nuts, milk, and eggs. Chances are that your child or one of their friends has a history of a food allergy. Reactions can be minor, like a mild rash where the food comes in contact with the skin, or they can be life-threatening. Children with a previous severe reaction to a food generally will have allergy testing and may know exactly what foods they should avoid. This is not something to take lightly — even small exposures can be deadly. Check out the Recipe Modifications on the next page to find alternatives to some of these allergy foods.

What can you do?

If you have a child with a food allergy, make sure that his teachers, coaches, and the school nurse all know about the allergy. If it is a severe allergy to a common food (milk for example) you should ask to have a meeting with the school principal to discuss how it will be handled in the lunch room and in the classroom. In general, awareness of the problem, and having a plan to deal with any reactions, are more important than elimination of the food from the school or isolation of the child.

If you are bringing a snack for a class or team sport, try to find out ahead of time whether there are food allergies among those children. If you can't find out ahead of time, think about bringing a low-risk snack for everyone or an alternative snack that doesn't have any nuts just in case there is a child with nut allergy. Many times parents will bring an alternative snack for their highly allergic child, but it is always appreciated when someone makes an effort to include a child who often has to eat a separate snack.

If you have a child with food allergies and discover a good modification for one of the recipes in the book, let us know and we'll post it on our website! **www.superkidsbook.com**